ALFREDO J LOPEZ

Karl, Friedrich and Us

Why Marxism Matters Today

First published by Entremundos Publications 2025

Copyright © 2025 by Alfredo J Lopez

Alfredo J Lopez asserts the moral right to be identified as the author of this work.

This work is released under a Creative Commons license. You may copy and distribute part or all of this book but you must attribute the used material to Alfredo Lopez as author, you must reproduce the text exactly as it is written and you may not charge for or financially profit from the distribution of that material.

First edition

ISBN: 978-1-877850-07-3

This book was professionally typeset on Reedsy. Find out more at reedsy.com

Contents

Prologue	1
Introduction	2
1 To Start	4
2 The Economy	16
3 The Society	33
4 Conclusion	59
Afterword	61

Prologue

One problem with writing books is that as you get older the part where you thank people gets longer. In formulating my own thinking, I am drawing from the lessons and contributions of people I've met, talked to and worked with for 60 years of activism and I meet, talk to and work with people every day. That's a whole lot of people.

So forgive my short-cut. I always thank my family — my two sons Karim and Lucas and my grand-daughter Alina — and my wife and life-partner Maritza Arrastia (the center of my life). This time I'll make specific mention of my colleagues at Media Justice because I was thinking of them as I wrote this and because they're amazing people who continue to teach me so much.

Then there's everyone I've ever spoken to and worked with. You know who you are and, if you're reading this, I mean it when I say "thank you".

Alfredo Lopez

Brooklyn, New York

June 19, 2025

Introduction

I decided to write this expanded essay when I was away at a retreat and a comrade/colleague of mine said, "I know lots of places to study Marxism but very few to study what it means to my work. My question isn't what Marxism says, it's why should I care." Now, for sure, there are such resources, good ones, better than anything I could write. But I'm at an age when I'm starting to think about what I'm leaving behind. After a lifetime of relying on Marxism to help me understand my world and my life and having written a bunch of books, I realized I've never written anything about Marxism per se.

So I'm writing this. I am not sure how helpful it will be to anyone but I owe it to the world to share a method of social analysis and vision of human society that has not only guided my own thinking but comforted me throughout my life. I don't know that this will be my last attempt to do this but it's my first.

My intention is to take what I consider the fundamental ideas that comprise Marxism and briefly look at how they relate to our current lives. This can't be exhaustive for a bunch of reasons including the instability and constantly shifting reality we are facing in this world. It's tough to describe the coffee when it's still percolating.

So I stuck to the basics. I've taken six concepts — the nature of people, the movement and creation of value, the society's base and super-structure, alienation, classes, and hegemony

— and I tried to link them to our current situation. That's what this short book is about.

My dream is for people to be able to read and discuss it in groups, use it as a tool of political education. But I'll be more than satisfied if people just read it and refer to it when needed. I love the idea of being there when you need to confer with me.

One quick note before you start reading this. This is not about movements or specific communities in struggle so there is scant mention of Global Majority people or LGBTQ+ people or women or the many other communities we can identify as impacted by oppression and critical to the struggle against it. Marx and Engels couldn't envision those populations' contribution and that's not my focus here. Believe, however, that these populations, their struggles and their leaders have had a huge impact on me and how I think and, in a refracted way, on the content of this work. You could say that everything I've ever written is about those populations and the issues that affect them.

After all, that's been my life and that's probably why I've been interested in Marxism throughout my adulthood: it explains my experience.

1

To Start

"I have a foreboding of an America in my children's or grandchildren's time — when the United States is a service and information economy; when nearly all the manufacturing industries have slipped away to other countries; when awesome technological powers are in the hands of a very few, and no one representing the public interest can even grasp the issues; when the people have lost the ability to set their own agendas or knowledgeably question those in authority; when, clutching our crystals and nervously consulting our horoscopes, our critical faculties in decline, unable to distinguish between what feels good and what's true, we slide, almost without noticing, back into superstition and darkness..."
Carl Sagan

- Why?

For most of my life, I've been contending with an assertion, popular within left-wing circles, that Marxism is irrelevant to understanding what we are and what we have to do.

It can be said that the more absurd an assertion, the more

difficult it is to refute and I think this is no exception. Not only is Marxism relevant today, it's necessary to understanding our lives and how to preserve and improve them. In fact, it's difficult to conceive of the current political and sociological "common sense" without Marxism's impact.

Yet, most people who are working for a revolution don't know Marxism and often think it's not relevant. In one way, that's understandable. The revolutionary movement in the U.S. is increasingly led by people of the "global majority" (aka "people of color") and frequently women and lgbtq+ people who have emerged from a tumultuous period of social and economic upheaval unlike any we have ever experienced. Marxist theory is based on the thinking and writing of two white guys, Karl Marx and Friedrich Engels, who lived in England during the 19th century: products of the period of developing capitalism, monumental social change and often violent struggle in a world that was dramatically different from ours in almost every way. How could their thinking still pertain?

The answer is that its pertinence is a product of its flexibility. Marx and Engels left us with a theoretical foundation for the analysis of a society: a base of sorts on which to develop a deep understanding of our own lives. What people call Marxism today is the work of a vast network of writers and activists who have used that foundation to develop a towering edifice of ever-morphing analysis. Marxism is, effectively, a collaborative project and that's what I want to talk about by explaining some of the basics of Marxism and how they might impact our lives today.

I want to identify some key concepts of Marxism, the ones I believe are essential to understanding what Marxism is all about, and I want to relate them to the developments that have reshaped our lives and sharpened our struggle for a future.

But first I want to take a short detour to introduce Marxism's founders.

By the way, I sometimes use their first names because that's how they addressed each other in letters — Yes, Marx really called him "Friedrich" — and also because it kind of makes me feel closer to them.

Karl and Friedrich

Fundamental Marxism is the work of Karl Marx and Friedrich Engels. Working in tight collaboration, they wrote a major three volume work, four other books, thousands of articles, speeches and letters (many of which were destroyed by Engels for security reasons). Through their work, they altered the way people viewed society at the time and shaped the way we see it today, and are now considered among the founders of social science and among the most influential thinkers in modern history.

Remarkable for its longevity, the quantity of collaborative work, and the quality of the thinking framed in that work, the relationship is equally remarkable for its very existence. They say that opposites attract and Karl and Friedrich were almost direct opposites in virtually every way.

Marx

Karl Marx was a ruffian. Poorly dressed, with what observers called a "swarthy complexion" and often wildly unkempt hair, he had an irascible manner, often displayed as an impatience bordering on arrogance. He was highly undisciplined in his work style; he rarely finished a piece he was writing on time and, even then, he would edit and re-edit it past deadlines as his roving mind encountered a new idea or nuance that had to be included.

Despite a prodigious output of writings, enough to fill a small library, most of what Marx wrote went unpublished during his lifetime.

He was a rebel and trouble-maker his entire life. As a student, he got into frequent trouble with the authorities for breaking windows and street lights after a night of drinking with his fellow "young Hegelians" (student adherents to the then audacious writings of philosopher George Wilhelm Friedrich Hegel). He clashed with police, fought with political opponents, got kicked out of classes in the various schools he attended and even fought a duel with a young Czarist officer over politics, an event he sometimes proudly recounted.

He was also poor for most of his life, living with his family in tenement apartments in various parts of London, which he rented under assumed names to hide from authorities chasing him. He scraped together enough money to survive through journalism, tutoring, and an allowance from his primary benefactor: Engels. The stability of his life was undoubtedly affected by the fact that Marx, for his last 30 years, was stateless. Although he lived in England for more than half his life, he never became a citizen.

Marx's love of alcohol and his constant smoking (mainly very cheap cigars) probably contributed to the many ailments he suffered for most of that life: severe liver and stomach problems, nausea, headaches, eye inflammation, neuralgia and rheumatic pains. Battling a nervous disorder which appeared around 1871, Marx began a steady intake of narcotics and the resulting nervousness meant he couldn't sleep well, would work far into the night and then spend the day recuperating in bed. All this was compounded by a horrible skin condition with infections to several areas of his body presenting as boils, a source of pain that frequently flared up and made it difficult for him to sit or stand upright.

Who knows? Maybe these physical challenges contributed to his personal combativeness. The certainty is that Marx made enemies and opponents of all kinds of people, particularly intellectuals with whom he disagreed. And he disagreed with almost everyone. Much of Marx's work is driven by often acerbic critiques of other thinkers and, in his activism, he was combative and demeaning of all opponents. To make matters more painful for his opponents he was usually right, because Karl Marx was a remarkable intellectual.

With an exhaustive command of philosophy in which he held a doctorate after finally having settled at one school long enough to earn it, he was also consummately knowledgeable about history and economics. He seemed capable of writing about everything in those three disciplines and frequently incorporated references to all three in his writings. Indeed, Karl Marx never accepted the idea that these three disciplines were separate except in the "foolish minds" of other writers and intellectuals of his day. He was also a novelist and playwright in his early days although, as time went on, he dropped those activities to concentrate on politics.

While Marx was probably not a very pleasant guy personally and disliked by many people in his political circles in London, he was a devoted and loving father and, by all accounts, his kids loved him back. Marx was faithful and loving to his wife and to his family.

And he truly loved Friedrich Engels.

Engels

It's as if nature set out to create Marx's opposing image. Tall for his time (about average height today) and the very picture of a European gentleman, Engels was always well dressed, courtly and of a "gay disposition" (according to several authors who met him). He was a frequent host of weekend gatherings of the radical intelligentsia which comprised his circle of friends. Mixing political conversation with the best wine and brandy of their day, they seldom broke up their gatherings before 2 or 3 in the morning. He loved conversation, was skilled at keeping things in a "friendly tone" and seems to have never made real enemies among other radical thinkers. Besides writing and organizing, Engels' main activities were of sport and leisure: riding, swimming and boating.

He was also rich. The son of a wealthy industrialist family, he inherited much of its wealth and eventually ended up owning one of the family's factories which he sold to a partner in 1870 at a handsome profit (dancing all the way home on the day of sale screaming, "I'm free").

Engels maintained several houses during his life, including a country estate. This was, in part, because he was under police surveillance for some of the time he worked with Marx; but there were also personal considerations. One of the homes he maintained was for his life-partner, Mary Burns, whom he never married out of principle (the belief that marriage is a form of slavery) but to whom he remained completely faithful under the equally strong belief that monogamy was an important virtue for a revolutionary. As a British gentleman, Engels could not risk the image of "living in sin" in his main house and would never risk his life-partner being scandalized. So he maintained a town-house he seldom slept in and lived in the one with Mary. When Mary died, he became involved with her sister Lydia and, as far as we know, these were the only two relationships he ever had. He never had children but was devoted to Marx's kids, who considered him almost a second father.

Engels, we are told, was a nice guy whose motto was "take it easy" — he actually wrote that in a self-description.

According to Marx's son-in-law, Paul LaFargue, Engels led "a double life" until he sold the factory. By day he was a highly efficient accountant and representative of his company, spending 10 hour days doing the books, overseeing production and writing to the company's many contacts all over the world. He was particularly suited to this task because Engels was one of history's greatest polyglots: fully fluent in Russian, Italian, Portuguese, Irish, Spanish, Polish, French and English (which he spoke and wrote impeccably) and able to converse in about ten more languages including Arabic and Polynesian.

After hours, however, he was a fervent revolutionary and that's what we remember him for. Founders of the First International in 1864 and drafters of the historic "Communist Manifesto" in 1847, Marx and Engels spent most of their collaborative time together doing lectures, writing pamphlets, keeping voluminous correspondence with revolutionaries all over the world and taking leadership positions in all the most advanced and active revolutionary organizations of their day. This was a partnership constructed of pure commitment.

It was also built of a true equality. The persistent myth is that Marx was an intellectual superior, the creative genius, while Engels was the obedient and efficient editor and "sponsor". In fact, they were intellectual equals although, as with much else, their intellectual interests and strengths often diverged.

While never achieving Marx's academic success or status, Engels wrote authoritatively about medicine, science, geography, topography, meteorology and literature to say nothing of his contributions to Marx's three favorite areas (economics, history and philosophy) that rivaled his collaborator's. Engels' frequent insistence that Marx was the "main thinker" was more a function of his generosity and humility than a statement of fact.

For instance, we know that Engels became a "scientific socialist" independent of Marx and was analyzing reality from a materialist and dialectical perspective (the approach most often popularly attributed to Marx) before they began working together. They got to that point walking separate paths. We also know that Engels' "editing" was much more than that: he frequently suggested different approaches, slightly different logic and examples that supported his changes to Marx's drafts and we know that Marx accepted many of those happily, telling Engels that his approach was the better one. In fact, Engels wrote the last two volumes of the duo's masterpiece, Capital, after Marx's death, using Karl's notes.

Finally, we know that a principal concept of Marxism — the primary role of the proletariat or industrial working class in revolutionary change — didn't come from Karl. Friedrich, who had just written a soon to be published study of the conditions of the British working class, convinced Marx of the idea during their first months of collaboration. In short, without Engels, Marx might not have taken the path we now know as Marxism.

The Duo

The bottom line is that it's simply not possible to examine the impact of their work without understanding it as the product of constant collaboration. For when those individually impressive minds came together, they forged an intellect that rivals any in human history, leaving a library of writing reflecting the partners' constant grappling with the issues they considered most important: how did the society in which they lived work and what was necessary to change it? Their efforts, constantly shifting and expanding as the years wore on and as their studies and collaborations broadened their thinking, form a seminal pillar of social science.

Isn't it ironic that their centrality is so universally accepted and yet so many people insist on arguing that their analysis is irrelevant to the world in which we now live? But when I explain to movement activists what I think are the essential concepts of Marxist thinking, the most common response is, "That's nothing new. Most sociologists say that." There is no greater testament to the sheer power of the fundamentals of Marx's and Engels' thinking. It's only when one looks at social analysis (including political economy) written before them, that the power of their ideas becomes clear: those ideas are "obvious" today but they were striking and controversial when they were first expressed.

The plaguing question, however, is how do they help us explain what's going on currently. So let's get started.

1 — What is a human?

(The Paris Manuscripts of 1844)

Marx and Engels' work is guided by the belief that all existence on Earth is dialectical: a constant, relentless series of clashes among things on the planet. These clashes, taking place every moment in the life of every single thing on Earth, change both things that are clashing. Essentially, our life is a process of development and all development is dialectical.

Karl and Friedrich would apply that understanding to their most important definition: the definition of what we are. Many people who seek to explain Marxism start with its economics but that skips a critical step because Marxist economics is based on a specific and revolutionary understanding of what some call "human nature." Without that, Marxism makes no sense.

Actually, Marx and Engels didn't use the term "human nature" because it implies a rigid, unchanging state and we are products, they said, of the dialectical clash between our drive to survive and the conditions that challenge that survival. That means this "nature" will be ever-changing, moment by moment, but it doesn't mean that there's no consistency. Like all living things, we are driven to survive and that drive's confrontation with reality produces what's special about us.

We are, compared to the rest of the world, a physically weak species: relatively small, very slow, pretty weak physically, poorly built to resist the punishment of our environment. So, from the start, we adopted the skill of collaboration because that was our only shot at survival. We do everything with others from hunting to thinking to growing things to building places where we can shelter and hide.

Other species do this, of course, but we have one attribute no other species has that makes our collaboration over-powering: we can see the future, we can imagine, we can think not only about what we now see and must do but what could be there and what we need to do to make it happen.

When Marx and Engels described "Gattungswesen" or "species essence" of humans (as Marx does in Economic and Philosophic Manuscripts of 1844 and the duo does in Capital) they stress this remarkable human quality: the ability to imagine the future. Developed over millions of years, made possible by the evolution of our complex memory system and the cognitive response to threats to our survival, this "skill" is the central pillar of human capability and forms the magnet holding together all of Marx and Engels' analysis. In Volume I of Capital, for example, they write about the brilliant collaborative work of bees in their hive as opposed to the not always successful work of an architect designing a building and then add, "...what distinguishes the worst architect from the best of bees is this, that the architect raises his structure in imagination before he erects it in reality." Imagination! The future! Of all living things on Earth, we are the only one that can envision a future, place ourselves in it and construct the things, ideas and experiences we are to produce before they even exist.

That remarkable capability is enhanced by two other critically important components to our "essence." First, humans have no natural enemies on Earth. We can actually co-exist with all life if we learn to respect and understand it. Second, there is no rational conflict of interest between any two humans or groups of humans. The conflicts we have, and there are many, are products of our own irrationality or that of the system we live under.

How do we apply these attributes to our survival? We build an economy, a way of organizing our collaborative work and the distribution of the things we make through that work into a system that assures our continued survival. Marxism is based on the idea that human society, the organization of human collaboration, is built around its economy, and everything, including government, culture, law, and social custom, develops in constant interaction with the necessities of that economy. To dispel a myth immediately, they never argued that economy dictates what happens in the rest of the society. Like everything else, it's dialectical. But the economy sets the frame for the development of everything else. It has to because, if not, the society would collapse.

But for most of human history, we just didn't have enough to feed everyone so the economy we have built, among the half-empty shelves of inadequate resource, has cast us into painful competition and crippling privilege. It created rich people and poor and infused the culture with class divisions and dominant class abuses. Essentially, it created capitalism and the greatest indictment of capitalism is how it contradicts and attempts to quash our "species essence."

To understand Marxism, it's essential to understand how irrational and destructive capitalism is and how this capitalist economy works and doesn't. That's a good starting point.

In essence, Democratic Party activist James Carville was right: "The economy, stupid!"

So…let's talk about the economy.

2

The Economy

2 — Commodity, Value, Circulation — Capitalism Simplified

(Capital, Volume I, "The Process of Production of Capital")

Among the most important and striking contributions Karl and Friedrich make to our understanding of our world is their explanation of how capitalism works, stressing the process of the creation and circulation of commodities as containers of "value". That's capitalism's motor and these guys kick off their masterpiece, Capital, explaining it in a deceptively simple and straightforward way.

The basic concept and terminology aren't new; a lot of people before Marx wrote about commodities, labor and value. Like in much of their work, however, Karl and Friedrich used the prominent thinking around them as a foundation for an explanation that departs radically from the up to then commonly accepted understanding.

Here's the rub though. Their explanation in Capital is abstracted to allow for its application in many contexts — Marx and Engels foresaw the many changes and adjustments that litter capitalism's history — and so it's not easy to understand at first read. For example, rather than speak of "money" or "profit" or "pay" which are basic elements of the simplified economics we see in news coverage today, they spoke of "value." In fact, that's the best way to see what they were saying but it's a bit abstract for those first encountering this analysis so, for the purpose of this explanation, I've used the terminology interchangeably based on what term I think explains things better. So, for example, value sometimes means "money." Bear with me. Ready?

Capitalism is driven by value. That's the gasoline in its tank and it's pumped by our labor. Work, the primary activity of the human race, creates value and the created value is held exclusively in commodities: goods or services created by labor and sold for profit.

This creation is a process that starts when the capitalist invests capital, or money, into production. He (it's usually a man) pays for a factory or workplace to be built or pays rent on it, buys raw materials for production, buys and maintains machinery for making stuff and then hires a bunch of people to work. These people are paid a wage for their labor and they are called "workers." That's a critical point: unlike most humans before capitalism, we're paid for our labor, not for the things we make or the services we offer. After all, most of us don't make a living selling our goods or crops at a marketplace and the capitalist really doesn't care what we're making as long as he can sell it. We are paid for working, by the hour, every day.

So that's our first interaction with the economy: we create

the value by making a commodity that holds it. That commodity then sits in a warehouse or store if it's a product or is part of someone's contract if it's a service. At this point, while holding the value, the commodity is also worthless because, to make money (i.e. realize value), the capitalist has to sell it. So the capitalist calculates how much money he's spent on its production and then adds some more money to make the price.

Then the thing has to be sold. The difference between the value initially stored in the commodity (sort of the money invested in making it) and the final exchange value (often expressed as the price) is called "surplus value" and its creation is the essential activity of capitalism. You can't have capitalism without it and everything capitalism does is aimed at increasing it. Its real-life version is reflected in what we call "profit." So surplus value is, in a sense, profit.

(It's also a sloppy translation which causes all kinds of confusion. Surplus is, after all, something not anticipated or not necessary and that's not what we mean here. The term in German Marx and Engels originally wrote is "added value" or "more value." Just store that one because, at this late point, nobody's correcting that translation. Back to sales...)

The sale of a commodity is called "the realization of surplus value" and there's a reason for that. If this thing isn't sold, it produces no profit and is absolutely worthless to the capitalist. Through capitalism's strange alchemy, it loses all its value. As obvious as that may now seem to us, it is a critical point because, in this formulation, Marx and Engels remove the economy from the realm of numbers and functionality. This isn't a self-perpetuating machine; it's an organization of human activity and, for it to work, every person in society must participate by buying the commodities we also make. For Marxism, capitalism is a human system requiring complete involvement of everyone in the society — a total buy-in. The systems of numbers written in black and red ink that many contemporary economists use to describe our economy and its fluctuations are only tracking the symptoms of a monumentally complex social interaction. We make everything and we buy everything and so "commodity value" is a creation of human labor throughout the entire process.

In fact, since this is the motor of society, labor can be viewed as the centrally important human activity under capitalism. We'll deal with how this affects politics and culture later but, for now, understand this: the value formulation developed by Marx and Engels over 170 years ago is a precise and accurate description of how our contemporary economy works and still the best one available. Understand it and you will understand capitalism, its functioning and its many contradictions and problems. In fact...

3 - The Principal Contradiction

(Capital, Vol. 3, "The Process of Capitalist Production as a Whole")

You may already be seeing a problem, sometimes referred to as "the principal contradiction of capitalism." If the capitalists are paying us a certain amount of money to make things and then add more to the price, how are we going to buy them? All the workers have is the money paid us. Of course, we don't buy the things we make exclusively but Marx and Engels didn't view production that way. They saw production, not as a bunch of products but as the result of the work of an entire class of people world-wide and that entire class buys everything it makes. So it can't afford all that it has made. In short, the system simply doesn't work. It's totally illogical.

Engels, after Marx's death, pointed out a further problem with capitalism in Volume III of Capital: what he calls "the tendency of the rate of profit to fall." It's a kind of cousin of the contradiction just explained. As capitalism develops, it becomes more able to produce stuff with less labor. Technology and advanced production increase the amount of goods produced, thereby dropping their price (making them less competitive). Makes sense: the more items you're selling, the lower you can charge for each item. But more product produced with less labor leads to displacing workers and shrinking the labor force. Sound familiar? While productive workers can't afford all we produce, displaced workers can't afford anything; they have no money.

Remarkably, Engels is picking up on the inherent contradiction that would show itself fully a hundred years after he wrote about it: the contemporary problem of mechanization and technology expansion that we're dealing with currently. It further condemns this system to an endless cycle of crisis.

It's just one example of how powerful Marxism actually is. It's not that Engels saw the future; it's that the future is a dialectical outcome of the present.

In any case, given these contradictions, this is a system destined for failure and the history of capitalism can be tracked through the efforts, by the capitalist class, to avert the impact of crisis and avoid failure.

4 - The Global Economy

(The Manifesto of the Communist Party)

"The need of a constantly expanding market for its products chases the bourgeoisie over the entire surface of the globe. It must nestle everywhere, settle everywhere, establish everywhere.

"The bourgeoisie has through its exploitation of the world market given a cosmopolitan character to production and consumption in every country. To the great chagrin of Reactionists, it has drawn from under the feet of industry the national ground on which it stood."

From the very start, Marx and Engels understood capitalism as a world system. This dictates how it acts as it exploits our labor but it also dictates how it contends with its own contradictions. In fact, those persistent contradictions and the crisis they create form the key to our understanding of how any of this is relevant to us because it is the one consistent element of capitalism's reality.

Capitalism functions each day not only to generate profit but to compensate for its persistent contradictions and hide its crises in the smoke of its politics. It was true back when Karl and Friedrich wrote about it and it's true today. To better understand this, let's do a quick summary of what "today's capitalism" looks like and how it's changed the society and our lives.

The world Marx and Engels wrote about was in the midst of an explosive growth in industrial production that society and government had not yet learned to manage. A capitalist could literally do anything he wanted with his workers; there were almost no laws protecting them. The borrowing systems were unregulated, framed by the policies of individual lenders with no governmental oversight. Contracts were written scantily. Property was frequently stolen (usually by the powerful). There was no living infra-structure (including sanitation) to speak of and very little health care for workers when they got sick as a result. In this primitive context, capitalism frequently veered out of control and that's a formula for collapse in a crisis-addicted system.

Things, of course, have changed. This country's labor movement (and that in much of the world) made monumental strides in creating protections for workers that were unprecedented, centering the idea that workers (rather than tools) were front-line participants in the processes of society's survival.

Those advances led to the creation of what was called "the middle class," an unprecedented and up to then unfathomable social construct that positioned a worker as the deserving beneficiary of a comfortable life-style and, more importantly, a certainty that this comfortable life would continue into the future. It is, after all, the future that is always in social contention. We can always survive what we face today but the question is how we handle what confronts us tomorrow. The entire history of social struggle is riveted to imagination and our belief in a future. Every gain made by the labor movement against the challenges of a worker's day and the quality of a worker's life is an act of imagination.

Capitalism has no imagination. As proven time and again by the statements of its apologists and oligarchs, this is a system that can't see beyond the weekly or monthly spreadsheet and can't lift itself off its bottom line. So it attacks the future as an unnecessary burden on its profit-seeking system, a harmful distraction. When not opposed effectively, it destroys everything workers have except the labor we can sell to the capitalist.

That's critical because, today in this country, the vast array of worker protections the labor movement won through tireless struggle have disappeared or dramatically decreased, chipped away by incessant ruling class attack. At the same time, the things we in the United States do for this system have changed as dramatically. We simply don't produce very much of anything anymore. The U.S and its G-7 partners (Canada, Japan, Britain, France, Germany and Italy) produce only about 26% of the global economy and that figure is dropping every year. In the complex system called a "world economy" our role is primarily consumption.

That leads some people to say that the classical Marxist model of production and consumption simply doesn't apply to contemporary U.S. society but that's wrong. It's a dwarfed reading of the process of value creation.

While we tend to view economies as "national" systems of exchange within the phony "nation states" borders, that's never been the way capitalism works. Even when it functioned primarily inside national boundaries, some fixed capital purchases (like raw minerals and materials) frequently came through importation from other places in the world. Marx and Engels point out that this international purchase would only expand. As the Communist Manifesto makes clear, they understood these primitive stirrings of the international economy as the presages of uncontrolled globalization. The century that followed their lives proved them right. It can be summarized as an era of inter-nationalization and today capitalism can only be understood as a world-wide system dominated by the ruling class of developed countries whose activity is constantly expanding.

There is obviously lots of production going on: all the stuff in your home is built by someone someplace. Your fruit and vegetables grow someplace. The vehicles that move you and your stuff are built in some factory, often merging components made in other factories in other countries. In short, you're still buying things and the things you buy are made someplace else.

It's no secret that this expatriation of production has happened, in part, to make production cheaper because workers in those countries frequently don't have the power to demand decent wages. But there are other reasons like the proximity to natural resources and, in many cases, very favorable arrangements between "foreign" companies and their national governments. The point here isn't to dissect or explain this "globalization" but to pose the question on the minds of revolutionaries, a logical version of the question Marx and Engels posed: given globalization, what kind of strategy do you pursue to make a revolution?

Part of the problem in coming up with an answer is that this globalization unfolds as capitalism in this country collapses because, bereft of production, our economy dangles on a thin thread of non-productive activity. Over a third of working people in this country work in commerce. Another third are in finance and service. In short, we work to sell to ourselves what others have produced and to manage the world-wide casino that is deceptively called "investment," gambling money on artificially bloated company stocks worth many times the real profit they yield.

Why is that "collapse?" Because, while our consumption keeps international capitalism alive, the lack of production means most people don't have a decent source of income. Our wages are now stagnant, the number of people in marginal employment has continued to grow, the number of people living in subsistence is larger than ever. Our species, reliant on its ability to see the future and feel the hopefulness that springs from it, now lives a culture of hopelessness based on very real criteria.

This is a new form of alienation, a topic Karl and Friedrich took up early in their collaboration and, like all forms of alienation, it's grounded in the economic conditions we face. While Karl and Friedrich could never describe this situation which is so far from the reality they confronted, they did anticipate that things could get to this point. This is why they stress the importance of consumption in the second volume of Capital. They also made space for an understanding of consumption in their study of society's structure especially their examination of the base and super-structure of our society which proved key to an understanding of how capitalism has survived this continuous mess.

5 - The Consumption Conundrum

(Capital Volume II, "the Process of the Circulation of Capital")

(Note: we're going to take up consumption as the necessary purchase of commodities. This is different than the "consumerism" that Marx and Engels frequently referred to as "consumption" which is a product of alienation that we take up later.)

During their lifetime, Marx and Engels were certain that revolution in the developed countries would be led by the proletariat as it seizes the means of production. In short, the struggle would be around workers' issues and the primary revolutionary action is taking control of the source of those issues: the machinery workers use to make commodities. They never viewed that as the total revolution — it's not clear how they saw that unfolding — but it was the spark, the defining pull of the social trigger, the step we need to take if we are to proceed on the path of revolutionary change.

We've never taken that step. Instead, the struggle has often been over issues of consumption, the other end of the cycle, and that obvious fact has been a source of angst for much of the organized Marxist movement in the U.S. In fact, among Marxist activists there has been a consistent reluctance to recognize the centrality of consumption accompanied by a stubborn insistence that, done right, the "proletarian revolution" continues to be key. We just have to explain why we got it wrong and how. Hence the angst.

Ironically, that gnashing of teeth is unnecessary because we didn't really "get it wrong". Capitalist society has changed as has this country's role in the world economy and our new primary role, as consumers, is no less important than our role as producers. Consumption, for Marx and Engels, was always as important as any other phase of value production. Today, it's even more important.

In contemporary United States, all political struggles are really about consumption: can I live sustainably and productively on what I get in this society and, if not, how do I get it? The protest of social groups like women, global majority people, LGBTQ+ people, disabled people and so many other populations may target prejudice, oppression, repression or denial (or usually a combination of all those) but at its root, it's about consumption. If women, for example, had full access to all they need to live a full, sustainable and productive life, the sexist stupidity of men would begin to fade. In fact, sexism isn't a function of attitudes, it's an exercise in power over what society commits to giving people. Erase the inequity in that and sexism, as we know it, would lose all purpose; it would simply fade away or become irrelevant or, at most, become some annoying attribute that can and should be ignored.

The reformist perspective is that oppression creates inequality; you hear that all the time. In fact, the opposite is true. Inequality, seeping from the pores of a dysfunctional economy, creates oppression and, in the dialectical dance that is human history, oppression increases inequality. Addressing the problem of inequality, by assuring adequate consumption, is the way to break the oppression cycle.

So, in the end, it's all about consumption...except when it's about democracy but, in a sense, it's the same thing.

For much of their common work, Karl and Friedrich held that material forces (including the economy) framed and greatly influenced the development of all aspects of human society. Engels would later give this a name: historical materialism. As we explained above, Marx and Engels believed that humans form societies to insure our survival and economies are the systems we develop to make that happen by organizing our labor and consumption. Everything else is built in dynamic reaction to that economy and through the constant dialectic among all society's institutions and forces.

In an elected democracy like this one, while political struggle is fueled by consumption, its target is almost always the government. Our protests almost always demand that our government do something or stop doing it. This changes further down the historical line when protest movements shift into revolutionary movements vying for power over the society but, for now, it's inescapable. Government is our target because we have been raised to expect that our government solves our problems and so the problems in our lives are seen as the government's failures. Advanced capitalism needs a sophisticated and highly engaging democracy to survive and one of its tenets is that all political activity takes place within the container of democracy and that all solutions to problems reside within the power of the government (or the state). To admit otherwise would set the political culture on an inevitable path to revolution.

It's logical then that one of the unique features of U.S. history is the tendency of democracy to expand and retract. While this takes place in other countries, it's never as explosively pronounced as it has been in this country with its history of continuous attempts to rewrite rights and democratic rules seeking to expand who votes, what we can say and do, where we can go and who we can do these things with...and a constant attempt to push back and restrict all that.

Marx and Engels were fascinated by U.S. democracy, going so far as to speculate that democracy might make proletarian revolution unnecessary. Marx wrote several articles about the U.S. Civil War and speculated, in letters, about how the democratic struggles taking place in the U.S. might eventually transform society. This was the only country in the world where Marx thought that possible. It's important to point out that Marx's naivete in this analysis could have been, in part, a function of his shallow understanding of the struggles of non-white peoples, particularly enslaved people in the U.S. Like many European men of his era, Marx suffered from a racial myopia that presented itself, on more than one occasion, as open racism. You can't understand democratic struggle if you don't understand racism. The struggles for democracy often mirror the sustenance struggles because the same populations are affected by both. It's a truism to say that black people, as an example, confront huge challenges in consumption while also having to fight every moment of their lives for the right to participate in democratic society, a right which is granted after struggle only to be taken away progressively after the fact.

The quagmire of contemporary politics is that, at this point, the government is fundamentally useless. With a Congress that is frozen by ridiculous partisanship and an Executive Branch that has spent the last 30 years coordinating military adventures and ignoring the increasing difficulties in the average person's life, our government can't be relied on to do anything positive. A movement of resistance whose culture centers on consumption and whose strategy centers on pushing the government to do its job is, essentially, doomed.

So what do we do? How do we take that step from mere protest, as effective and important as that can be, to genuine revolutionary struggle? There's the problem. If Karl and Friedrich told us very little about how to make a revolution based on production, they didn't even think about making one based on consumption. Sure, they understood its importance to capitalism's functionality but they didn't consider its revolutionary importance because they believed production would drive the revolution. In any case, it wasn't Karl and Friedrich who gave us the strategy for production-driven revolution, it was the revolutionaries who followed them, the people who actually led revolutions who developed the strategy for it. While the success of these efforts, whether centered on factories or farms, was ersatz at best, there has never been a consumption-based strategy and that's logical because the centrality of consumption presents us with major challenges. Gone is the "unity of place" that workplace organizing always provides: giving us places for meetings, idea sharing, and productive informal conversation. If we are to organize around consumption, how do we do it? Revolutionary history has provided many lessons in consumption organizing but none of these forms of organization afford us the bridge to revolutionary action that workplace organizing does. At the workplace, you take over the means of production and you're in power...or close to it. In the community, you take an action and...what?

If I had to name one major failure of the revolutionary movement in this country it would be the inability to develop a strategy based on the importance of consumption. Marx, Engels and the revolutionaries who followed them gave us a strategy logically flowing from the ascendancy of production in the developed countries. While that strategy has proven unavailing, it at least gave us a foundation for strategic conversations about the future. But when production gave way in importance to consumption as the primary human activity, we failed to come up with even that start of a strategy. As a result our work was relegated to reformist struggles that, while critically important and often productive, failed to forge a road to the greater goal of revolution.

Things are now complicated by recent developments in the economy that may change the picture even more. Some thinkers, like the Greek activist/economist Yanis Varoufakis, argue that we are now in a new system run, not by production or consumption, but by the data gathering and storage functionalities of information technology and the few companies that control it. In his latest book, Techno-Feudalism, he argues that the ascendancy of this data technology has actually replaced capitalism as our primary mode of value creation and that today, everything we do in interaction with the economy is using the "feudal estates" of the data company owners like Elon Musk and Mark Zuckerberg. They are the vassals; we're the peasants, all of us including major capitalist company owners. While it's tough to accept that this formulation summarizes our complete reality, it certainly reflects a significant part of it and may map our general direction into the future.

What's your day like? Even the most technophobic among us spend most of our day interacting with information technology. We shop with it, bank with it, keep appointments and maybe even have appointments with it, make all kinds of life-style and consumption choices with it, deal with our governments with it…everything is in the hands of these data-controlling giants. You can't argue with that although it's true that much of this facilitates the operations of capitalism as we know it — the thing Karl and Friedrich wrote about. You go on-line to shop for anything you want, usually through Amazon and Amazon is a giant facilitator for the sale of commodities: it helps create surplus value.

The problem however is that these data companies control the economy in ways that are completely different from capitalism at any stage. They aren't driven by the production and consumption of those products although they survive because that happens. Rather they are driven by the rental income they get from capitalists and the payments they get for their information, like what Google amasses about your buying habits which is why when you Google something you immediately see ads that cater to what you may have searched for or bought from Amazon in the past. How do they know that? They keep your search data by tracking your searches; they get your purchase data from

Amazon. These companies buy your data from each other.

Why is any of this important? After all, capitalism is still very present and without it the rest crumbles. We aren't just examining capitalism, however; we're looking to replace it through revolutionary action. How do you do that with this data empire? The simplicity of means-of-production-take-over, which may have been illusory even during Marx and Engels' day, is no longer available to us. We need a brand new strategy.

3

The Society

6 — Base and Superstructure — What, How, Who?

(Introduction, A Contribution to the Critique of Political Economy — Karl Marx)

In a university class I was teaching a while back, a young woman was raising the problem of lack of available men. Yes, she explained, the fellows did ask her out and she did, in fact, date but she would never go out a second time with a man who wasn't wearing a shirt that looked brand new. Clearly this had become a problem because her social life was extremely limited but, she insisted, "If his shirt isn't brand new, what does that say about his respect for me?"

Many in the class found her logic comically curious and, looking back, I still find myself laughing at her grotesque extremism but then I check myself with a question. Was her thinking all that strange or was it merely the logical extension of a ubiquitous and tenacious social prejudice: that the clothes you wear reflect some quality you have or success in life or... well...anything other than the fact that you're protecting your body from the elements.

We call this a fetish: attributing life-impacting powers to an inanimate object. You find these in all kinds of religions all the time. But, because of its prominence, this fetish with clothing nourishes a component of an over-all vision of society through which our ruling class continues to rule. It's the idea that we, individually, can attain a life of abundance and security and, when we don't, it's our fault. We didn't say the right things, learn the right things, do the right things and, yes, dress in the right things. There is no alternative to this reality that we experience as individuals, alone and isolated. We can't escape it; we don't even want to. We can call this the "narrative" and it's part of what Marx and Engels called "superstructure" which is vital to capitalism because it's part of the arsenal this chronically ill system uses to stay alive. Its role is to frame the ideology of capitalist society we are pressured to buy into; other superstructural elements like the state are there to make sure we capitulate to that pressure.

There's an oft-repeated criticism of Marx and Engels: that their focus on the economy ignored important social and cultural forces molding our society and lives. You often hear that from left-wing activists explaining why they reject Marxism: it doesn't address so much of what makes us tick and oppresses us.

While it's true that Capital, their masterpiece, stays away from many of these sociological and cultural forces, that's probably because it's a work strictly about the economy and how it works. Marx and Engels address everything we face in our social lives through other works and their thinking is summarized by Marx in *A Contribution to the Critique of Political Economy* which is a study of the various strands of political economy published during their time. It articulates an idea that is the foundation of Marxism: "It is not the consciousness of men that determines their being, but, on the contrary, their social being that determines their consciousness."

This is a critically important question right now because the centrality of consumption in our daily lives literally defines those lives. In capitalism, consumption is tied inextricably to culture and, in many cases, capitalism's need to nurture consumption and expand it actually forms how we think about ourselves. Let's track that but, first, let's define what we need to do the tracking: the societal frame they drew generally referred to as "base and super-structure".

For Karl and Friedrich, "the base" is the economy and the " operational laws" that govern it: pretty much the formula of commodity production, circulation and consumption we just covered. You might call this the motor of capitalist society.

The "super-structure" is just about everything else: that complex weave of political, social and cultural forces that guide the societal vehicle the motor is moving. We'll take a look at that now.

7 - Flimsy Consciousness

(Prison Notebooks, Antonio Gramsci)

While super-structure is essential to capitalism's functioning, Marx and Engels didn't spend a lot of time writing about it.

Other than that basic treatment in *A Contribution to the Critique of Political Economy*, the concept gets little more than an occasional mention, mainly a parenthetical remark, in their other work. That's probably because they felt it more pressing to understand the economy and how its failings would drive revolution or maybe they just didn't have enough time. In any case, the absence of analysis of super-structure makes it important to read and study the work of the guy who picked up where they left off: an astounding thinker, the Italian communist leader and my favorite Marxist, Antonio Gramsci.

Gramsci was a political comet: all his work was done in a life ending in his early forties, his body ravaged by illness and disability exacerbated by the brutal repression he suffered at the hands of the Italian government. Under five feet tall, extremely thin and hunched over, he was hardly an over-whelming physical presence. But he brought to Marxism an analysis that thrust it into the 20th century and beyond, presenting a picture that is not only relevant today but absolutely necessary to understanding where we are and how we got here.

Because Gramsci was a revolutionary leader and a front-line activist, much of his analysis, mostly written in jail, dwells on how to make a revolution and why we haven't done so yet. Part of his answer to that vexing question is an expansion of Marx's formulation that people's "social being determines their consciousness." Sitting in his prison cell, he posed a critical question: how does this socially determined consciousness impact our will to make a revolution? His answer is that the consistent failure of revolutionary effort in developed countries is due, not only or even mainly to the repression of the state, but to capitalism's ideological hegemony over us. We are part of a super-structural consensus based on a narrative shared by working people that accepts capitalism's explanations and self-defenses. In short, capitalist society is built on and protected by our acquiescence. So, if you're going to make a revolution, he argued, you have to develop an alternative narrative: a consciousness about ourselves and our lives, a "proletarian culture."

Try to visualize, as one message, all the messages you receive about your life every day. It's conveyed in many ways: advertising (a big one), statements of people in authority, official pronouncements, media content...so much more. What do this society's most powerful people want you to believe about yourself: what is the self-image that is being offered to you daily?

To sum it up: you're powerless...alone...living a horrible life and unable to do anything about that. To address your problems, you need "them" and the stuff they can sell you. So the ad you saw today insists that, by wearing a particular chemical on your body, using a specific utensil, or buying a particular brand of cereal, you can improve your life. All advertising is about your deficiency and how, through consumption, you can address it.

The same is true in the messages you receive about authority. Even when a propagandist (usually a journalist) acknowledges that something is wrong with our society, the option offered is to vote. While voting might be a tactical choice for some, it can't possibly be the main action of choice for those seeking fundamental change because the electoral system as currently constructed is part of the thing we want to change. That's why, although all change starts with mass action that is extra-judicial and often extra-legal, those options are never floated by the propaganda machine. Through their multi-faceted idea machinery, the capitalists tell us to register and vote if we want change.

These message machines form the mechanism of the narrative construction, the ideological hegemony talked about, and they are the most important part of the contemporary repressive apparatus. Indeed, while a specific country can tamp down revolutionary activity through the physical might of its state, the capitalist class as a whole with its sweeping authority over so many countries, can't hope to do that. Repression is sloppy, prone to push-back, insubstantial, insecure and fragile. If you really want to rule in a complex capitalist society for any significant length of time, you have to do it through hegemony.

The proof of the power of the hegemonic dance is the fact that, while everything indicates that capitalism has collapsed and is useless and toxic, most people in the United States can't conceive of another type of society; they can't envision revolutionary change. It's not that they are opposed to it; they just can't fathom it.

A primary tool of this obfuscation is the shimmering image of "successful life" that we mentioned above and that's driven home by advertising and every other propagandist mechanism at capitalism's beck and call. Capitalism dedicates enormous resources, entire populations of workers, years of cultural formation and minute by minute social messaging to conveying this message, so essential to capitalism's survival and manages to weave the message into the daily conduct of our lives. Nowhere is this more clear than in the fetishistic consumption that not only saves our economy but actually defines our culture.

In their path-breaking book *Monopoly Capital,* economists Paul Sweezy and Paul Baran situated marketing as a primary tool capitalism uses to deal with one of its most crippling permanent problems: at this point in our history, we don't need most of what we buy and if we stop buying, capitalism collapses. So how are they going to get us to buy what we don't need? To re-use the clothing example: How much clothing do you really need? To maintain cleanliness of your clothing, you need two changes and only need to buy more when one of those changes falls apart from age. Now, look at your closet. Why in the world have you bought all that clothing?

Whether we admit it or not, as pointed out above, most of us treat clothing as an indication of our success, quality, attractiveness and usually a combination of all that and more. It is, in our culture, a magic wand through which we can conjure a safe and secure life. Clothing is our protective layer against the ravages of hopelessness.

We probably do this sub-consciously, almost reflexively. When we do actually think about clothing, it is usually in relation to others: we dress to attract, to impress, to dazzle, to make a statement, to self-define before others. Our clothes are among the most powerful things we have. Yet as a fetish they have no real power.

Here is a case where a fetish that yields enormous hegemonic power also pays off in profit because clothing is a major part of our economy. Food, luxury items and technology function in much the same way: giving us stuff we don't need but are dying to buy because our culture has taught us that having these things makes for a successful life and the more we have of them, the more successful we are.

In the end, it all proves vaporous; you aren't happier because you have a lot of clothes or because you eat lots of expensive food or have a house full of things that do stuff you don't really need for your survival. You buy these things, you own them and then...nothing. They become an accepted and pretty useless part of your life. Like any addiction, their acquisition merely leads to your desire for more.

The motor that drives this fetishism, an imposed consciousness that stresses our individuality, relative powerlessness and pursuit of an impossible happiness, is actually flimsy because it's debunked every moment of our lives as we travel from one painful disappointment to another. But it proves resilient; we see it refuted today even as we continue to believe in it. Capitalist culture blinds us to the obvious. To remain in power, our ruling class depends on us not paying attention to our lives, not thinking about them, being distracted by useless activity. Most of capitalist culture's most popular past-times involve activities that bring us little knowledge or real life experience or even true joy. They are merely distractions whose impact lasts as long as we're doing them.

The irony of fetish consumption's central role in capitalist hegemony is that it is actually fundamental to the economy and, as such, a major issue in the development of revolutionary strategy.

8 - ...but why the fetish...why the weakness?

(The Economic and Philosophic Manuscripts of 1844)

Marx and Engels wouldn't be surprised at the extent to which fetishism has overtaken us. They saw it as an ever-increasing disease connected, in a sense, to the primary affliction we suffer: alienation.

There is still, among contemporary Marxists, a tendency to dismiss Marx's treatment of "alienation" as an early foray into a kind of humanistic left thought that these writers say was later corrected when Marx and Engels became full time economists. Put another way, Marx said stuff about alienation in 1844 and then never repeated it, which would indicate that he either didn't care about it or had changed his thinking on it.

That makes no sense and belongs, with all the talk about "early and mature Marx", in the intellectual wastebasket. While it's true that Marx and Engels later work centered on "economics" that's probably because they were writing Capital, whose length and scope is larger than anything else they had ever written. Throughout all their work, however, there's an understanding of alienation and its impact on people's lives and behavior starting with Marx's remarkable description of alienation in the Economic and Philosophic Manuscripts of 1844, also known as the Paris manuscripts.

In his mid-twenties, the young Marx was constantly on the move, having been effectively expelled from Prussia. He went to Paris, the center of European left thought at the time, and met a bunch of the top left-wing intellectuals of his day: the foundational anarchists Mikhail Bakunin and Pierre-Joseph Proudhon, one of the fathers of cooperative politics Louis Blanc, the great lyricist and poet Heinrich Heine, the political economist Pierre Leroux and, of course, Engels himself. Sitting at large tables in Parisian cafes, these thinkers would pass around their latest writings for collective critique and energetically discuss their differences.

Out of these collaborations, young Karl got the idea of writing a bunch of pamphlets on various topics refuting Hegel's work and ideas. Like most of what he wrote, they were never finished and, in fact, went unknown until 1932 when scholars in the Soviet Union discovered and published the notes and first drafts

Marx had written. The publication shook the Marxist world because, since Karl's death, many Marxists had projected their thinking as "purely scientific" and devoid of any "personal or emotional" touch. The '44 manuscripts are loaded with those kinds of touches and they prove, without question, that what always motivated Karl Marx was the pain people experienced under capitalism. He was a true revolutionary raging at the systemic oppression he saw all around him.

This is clear in Marx's understanding of alienation. In three paragraphs of the manuscripts, he explains how life for a worker is a multi-dimensional nightmare of denial.

Workers, he explains, are alienated from the product of our labor because, for the first time, we don't own the product we actually make. All we now own is our labor which we sell to the capitalist.

We are alienated from our own activity because our labor is now reduced to mindless repetition like that of an assembly line, doing the same thing over and over all day long and never seeing the result or being able to enjoy the feeling of accomplishment a finished product would bring.

We're alienated from the species-essence ("Gattungswesen") we spoke about before. We are, by nature, prone to multi-faceted interests, constantly tying activities together in our minds, drawing comparisons and relationships and thinking about the future. This is the source of our boundless potential. But this natural tendency is frustrated by capitalism's limiting mechanical demands on us which make all that imaginative adventure unimportant and even "distracting." For the capitalist, our tendency to think creatively is a deficiency and a waste of our time. In fact, given our potential, the time-waster is the work the capitalist forces us to do.

Finally, we're alienated from other human beings because our work is isolated from them and, too often, in direct competition with theirs. Our labor is a product that competes with others' labor on the shelves of capitalist compensation. The product we produce which creates the value from which we are compensated competes with other similar products made by people with the same needs for compensation. Our nature is to collaborate and we are the most collaborative animal on earth; that's how we have survived. Capitalism forces us to act in the opposite way.

Your life, under capitalism, is a series of compromises that crush your happiness: a constant scramble to "escape" the regular pain of your daily life or seek out slim pockets of pleasure in what is, otherwise, a painful world. That's because of alienation and it doesn't have to be that way; society can be good.

This inability on our part to access the potential of a good life has accumulated over the generations and it mars and distorts us. With ever-greater frequency, the alienation that affects us grows to envelope our lives and we live a culture of constant division, insecurity and hopelessness. Young people are increasingly unable to envision the future.

In my last book, *Goodies from the Yum Yum Tree*, I tried to describe this alienation as a "feeling" this way:

"You fear losing everything. You fear disaster visiting your family, community or country. You fear the ominous presence of catastrophic disease wrecking your life and that of those around you. You fear walking the streets or failing at new experiences or not living up to the potential you or others believe you have. You fear not being loved or liked or respected. You fear for the future of your children or the children of your friends.

"You fear what some man looking at you might do and so you

spend time agonizing over what the last one did. You fear white people and how deeply they hate you. You fear people who aren't white and how rapidly they are taking over your world.

"You fear that, contrary to what you've been taught, there is no benign presence watching over your life.

"In confronting this fear, however it presents itself, you feel alone. That is the greatest fear you can have. Being alone painfully contradicts the most fundamental of human instincts: the need to be connected with others."

The volcanic spread of information technology in our lives has amended this classic alienation. We live information technology. It's impossible to avoid it. As it envelops us as an entire connected humanity, it isolates each of us physically. Because our primary contact is through bytes of computer code, we are alienated from the physical contact with others. Because we can live apart from our physical bodies and daily realities, constructing a false on-line persona, we are alienated from ourselves. Because information technology makes privacy rights virtually impossible to enforce, we are alienated from our own lives, their uniqueness and their legitimate integrity.

This is the current version of alienation made possible by the rise in mass consumption but the specifics stay within the frame that Marx and Engels laid out for us. The classic forms of alienation paint a picture of a society that separates us from our basic "species essence": our need for social collaboration, our ability to see the future and construct it, our sense of self-worth. All of these are under attack in this "new alienation" as well. While the specifics have changed the impact is the same and alienation remains a major obstacle to revolution, a fact our left has consistently ignored in its work and analysis. We've always been taught and have come to believe that the mere presentation of political realities would flood people's consciousness with logic that overcomes the craziness of alienation. Just get the opportunity to have a sober discussion with someone and you'll convince them and they'll somehow divest of all this fear. But it doesn't happen most of the time.

Instead, we elect Donald Trump, and dip ourselves into some bizarre paranoid fantasy in which everyone around us becomes a potential threat. The feeling I described in *Goodies* has now become one of the themes of contemporary politics. Karl and Friedrich would have nodded and shrugged: alienation is a product of the economic relationships that govern our society and, as our economy tanks, the economic relationships and alienation intensify. See how each of those forms of alienation has deepened during the last 20 years?

Before we get to a brief look at the society we currently live under, which is our final chapter, we need to touch on one other topic.

9 - Classes

(The Manifesto of the Communist Party, Karl Marx and Friedrich Engels)

No Marxist concept is more misunderstood than class. It's linked by most people in our society, and many in our movement, to virtually every facet of human behavior, life-style and involvement. Class, the way Marxism understands it, has nothing to do with any of that.

In part, the problem was attaching a morality to class, as if it were someone's choice to be in one, a personal fault. During my early movement days, calling someone "petite bourgeois" was one of the biggest insults conceivable, and just about everyone who lived in a neighborhood of five-story buildings was part of the "lumpenproletariat" (a fact of which to be proud).

In their social analysis, in which class plays a seminal role, Karl and Friedrich never put a value on class. They certainly judged what the classes did during capitalist production but that was never personal. Engels, for instance, was a scion of a capitalist family — effectively a member of that class. For Marx and Engels, you are a member of the class you were born into and how you deal with that is the purpose of your life.

What's more, class isn't about how much money you have or where or how you live. It's about only one thing: your relationship to the means of production.

For Marx and Engels. a class is a group of people who share common economic interests, are conscious of those interests, and engage in collaborative action to advance those interests. Karl and Friedrich said that the basis of construction of these classes is capitalist production or its "means".

Traditionally, if you own the means of production and that production generates more capital than you need to run your business, you are part of the bourgeoisie. In short, you hire people to work for you and they make products that generate enough money for you to save and invest. Period.

If you work for a living and depend on the wages you make to survive, you are part of the working class (or what Marxism often calls "the proletariat").

Those are the two classes of importance, and in the *Communist Manifesto*, Marx and Engels say, "Society as a whole is more and more splitting up into two great hostile camps...Bourgeoisie and Proletariat."

There are a couple of other "smaller classes" that original Marxists said would fade away quickly and just aren't all that important.

If you own a business of some kind that generates about enough to keep itself afloat but doesn't really generate profits you can save or re-invest, you're a petite-bourgeois: small business owner or owner of a professional firm of some kind.

If you live detached from normal capitalist production — are chronically unemployed or live off behavior that would normally be considered crime — classical Marxism calls you "lumpenproletariat". That requires a bit of explanation, however, because some Marxists (myself included) don't believe this "class" exists. People normally grouped as lumpen do, in fact, have a deep and abiding relationship to the means of production because they buy stuff and, as we've said, that is the primary value-creation activity in this society. Most "workers" don't produce commodities in this country so why label these people something different?

Like almost everything associated with Marxism, all this requires an update. The change in the importance of consumption over production has to alter our views of class since it's the production process that frames classes originally. This is a very new development and it's still percolating so, at best, we can point to some directions. What can be said confidently is that, aside from these traditional classes, there are now "social groups" that are, effectively, new classes.

Subaltern

It was Gramsci who first posed the idea that colonialism has had an impact, not only on the economy, but on the classes that function within it and he posed the concept of a new class he called the "subaltern". This is a colonized group that, rather than dominated by the oppressors in the political discourse, is actually excluded from that discourse entirely. This happens in the colonies but it also takes place when that colonized population moves to the metropolitan centers. As a result, these populations develop their own narrative, culture, language and world view and the hegemonic power that manipulates the society is weaker over them...sometimes bereft of influence. That's why so many of them end up in jail; it's the only way society can control them.

I'm not going into that much more except to say that the revolutionary movement in this country has never developed a strategy that includes the subaltern. In fact, we have traditionally neglected them and left their organization to liberal activists. For far too long, we misidentified this group confusing it with the lumpenproletariat Marx and Engels so disparaged.

But the subaltern is no such thing. While the lumpenproletariat has no economy separate from the leeching it does off the working class, the subaltern develops its own economy, frequently separate and often actually legal and . From street vendors to unlicensed repair specialists to the armies of construction workers one sees lining up early mornings to get picked up by contractors for a day's labor...this subaltern is very separate from the regular working class but is essential to our economy and, perhaps, to our social future.

Elders

One of Marxism's achievements is to remove the idea of "aging" from the mystical, almost magical context in which it's frequently viewed to an understanding of aging as a dialectical interaction between our body and our environment. All life is impacted by that interaction.

What's powerful about this understanding is that it centralizes society and the social problems we face as catalysts of our aging. The fact is that, scientifically, our bodies don't have to die. There is no internal time clock ticking us toward the final breath, no meter that measures where we are and tells us when we're finished. Organs do not automatically fail "from use" in and of themselves. The use of our body is in interaction with the world. Every movement you make is "against" some obstacle, every moment of your life pulls the air around you into your lungs, exposes your skin to the temperature and elements, forces your mind to grapple with the enormous complexity of your life and demands from your heart the strength needed to deal with all that. It's not life that wears your down; it's life in this society.

Of course, that will always be true and there will never be a society that assures eternal life. Life is hard no matter what society you live in. But it's much harder under capitalism than it has to be. Capitalism forges a brutal, cruel society and, in the dialectic that is civilized life, that brutality and cruelty makes us old.

While old people have always been present, and noticed, in human society, the concept of "elder" or "older person" or "senior" is a social construct of the capitalist period of development. Capitalism demands healthy bodies in its workers and, when its punishment wears the body down, it seeks to discard the person as a socially valuable being. As elders, we produce less and consume more.

We've never viewed elders as a class but the central importance of consumption means that elders, as a group, have a defined role in value creation and the possibility of social change. Over 35 percent of the people in the United States are elders, over

60 years old. While their income and potential for consumption reaches across a spectrum, the uniformity in these people's lives is striking. Denied sustainable income, due to the slashing of social security and the inadequacy or absence of retirement income, our elders are pressured to purchase goods from a specific product group that no other social group needs: survival goods. From walking aids, to wheel chairs, to compensatory vision or hearing aids to cabinets of various medications, the elder consumption group has created an entirely new branch of product for capitalism. At the same time, it's age, insecurity and the period of its development makes this group more accepting of social structures and less rebellious. It votes, acts and talks conservatively to a larger extent than any other demographic.

The Tech Oligarchy

Not all the "new classes" are oppressed or exploited. We are now seeing the growth of what looks like a new "ruling class": the tech oligarchy.

For most of capitalism's history, the bourgeoisie has been our ruling class and it's still the dominant class: really rich and powerful and in control of much of life. But there is a new class within capitalism that is voraciously and rapidly consuming power. Some call it the "broligarchy" and it's comprised of a relatively small group of white men who run those technology companies we were talking about above.

The rise of this new class isn't incidental. In fact, this group of men has quickly assumed control of much of capitalism's functionality and are now in leading positions of the U.S. government and state. They have, literally, taken over in the U.S. As they quickly expand their power over our lives, what do we do to push back and eventually overthrow them? What strategy do we need here?

(For a deeper dive into the bros and their tech, inappropriate in this space, I'd recommend the Media Justice tool box and presentations. They are as good as things get on this topic. Yanos Varoufakis' book *Technofeudalism: What Killed Capitalism* is also worth reading and a "fun read," by the way.)

10 - The Trump Lesson

(Prison Notebooks, Antonio Gramschi...Capital, Karl Marx and Friedrich Engels)

In 2025, Donald J. Trump won his second term as President of the United States and commenced what could be called a scorched earth policy: closing several major federal government agencies, firing large numbers of workers in others, bullying universities, media and institutions of learning to drop their study of the history of African heritage people in this country, using military force against lawful demonstrations. It frontally and brazenly attacked activists, particularly those non-citizens who held resident status, and began extorting large amounts of " time" from large firms who had either opposed Trump or an ally in court in the past or hired someone who he didn't like. It has now launched criminal investigations and arrests against political opponents including judges and elected officials. It has engaged in a frantic attack against international students at universities. The United States has never seen anything like this.

Since so much of this bore no resemblance to the "Make

America Great" program he had promised during his campaign, many people were shocked and confused. What in the hell is this guy doing?

Things were made worse by a bizarre set of measures: the assignment of trade tariffs to virtually every country that did any business with or in the U.S. It was an act that every economist of all political stripes opposed and most said it was simply insane.

But it's not. Certainly President Trump displays every symptom of mental instability and is a vicious, ignorant man. But, while he makes the decisions and announces the actions, he isn't designing the strategy, and identifying those who are doing the design may help us understand what they're seeking.

We're really at the start of the mess as I write this so any analysis is going to be speculative at best but there are parts of this administration that are long-term and will present difficulties for a very long time.

Not only are we in "early days" but we don't have much theoretical work to rely on in understanding this situation. I cited Gramsci because, in his newspaper articles, prison notebooks and speeches to the Italian legislature, he tracked and then denounced Italian fascism, something most parties of the day (including opposition parties) refrained from doing. So he's important but he's not entirely helpful because the conditions under which fascism rose in the past are fundamentally different from those of today. Rather than seek a secure dock in past Marxist writing, maybe we can use Marxist methods to build ourselves a new one.

The systemic transition from a collapsing "monopoly capitalism" to an under-regulated and sometimes unhinged "techno feudalism" (as Varoufakis calls it) has provoked a very serious internal conflict within the ruling class of this country. As the

the U.S. social edifice collapses under the weight of too long deferred contradictions, tech oligarchs contend with fascist ideologues as opportunist finance capitalists flip and flop politically — all of them trying to influence outcomes. None are capable of any long-range vision, so the apparently twisting and often self-contradictory thundershower of harmful policies show themselves to be nothing more than quick responses to an immediate perceived or imagined problem. The long-term impact never seems to be weighed. It's a literal madhouse.

It's important, however, to understand that this madness, as it were, is only the logical outcome of capitalism's fast-burn decline as it reaches this final stage. Weighed down by debt, ballooned by financial speculation, unable to reverse the horrifying world-wide trend of increasing under-nourishment, oblivious to the complete destruction of the Earth's climate, battered by but addicted to constant war (the source of both pain and profit) this is a system that's finished. Economies exist to meet a society's needs. Although this one has never done that completely, it now no longer does it at all.

We can't rely completely on Marx and Engels here. Certainly they foresaw the disaster that the collapse of capitalism would bring; it's in the formulas and formulations running through all their work, particularly Capital. This great system, they held, was born sick, suffering the illness of its contradictions and it won't recover. It will die and probably take us with it. The one survival act we have to save us from that death is revolution and Marx and Engels were certain the working class would make one in time. Not foreseeing that revolution not happening might not be a failure given the times in which they lived but, given the impact it has on us, it is certainly their greatest weakness.

So we have to do most of this work ourselves as the collapse of this system creates the political mess that is the ruling class's inescapable crisis. It's also a profound disappointment for the rest of us. Hegemony isn't a surface ailment; it seeps into the deepest part of our consciousness and secures our intellectual lives. Those lives become insanely unhinged when its primary assertion, that capitalism is the key to tomorrow's success, fails.

As a species that can envision the future, humans must by necessity depend on there being one. We are calm today only when we can be confident of tomorrow, even if that confidence is false. We are now unable to be confident of anything and, as would any animal, we frantically turn to the simplest outcome, the most visible "problem", the thing we have been trained to blame. That's how fascism erupts and, in the United States, it has erupted.

There is one bright spot in the picture. We're talking about the human race and the human race has, with it remarkable ability to see tomorrow, consistently shown genius in devising ways to survive. With 8.5 billion people collaboratively thinking of the solution, we can confidently believe one will arise.

11 — The Alternative

(Karl Marx, "the *Civil War in France*")

At some point in their collaboration, Marx and Engels faced a monstrously sobering fact: as "logical" as revolution was for the proletariat, the proletariat wasn't making one. Some say that this is the reason the pair took up the writing of Capital: to explore this system, its contradictions and the social framing emanating from it because that's the first step in planning a revolution.

But what if the problem wasn't workers opting for revolution as a step? What if the problem was that workers had no idea what would follow the step? Would you risk your life and turn reality upside down for a future you could not foresee? Why make a revolution if you don't know what the revolution will create? That was a problem then and it's a huge problem now.

For all their speculation about how a revolution could take place, Marx and Engels spent very little time describing how we could govern one. The closest they come to describing a socialist government in a society is their treatment of the Paris Commune in 1871. Marx himself collected piles of newspapers, magazines, letters, leaflets and pamphlets — literally everything he could get his hands on — to study the Commune and analyze it in laudatory and almost giddy tones.

That the Commune lasted six months is less important than what it provided Marks and Engels. Here, they saw a city-wide government run, essentially, by the working class in respectful collaboration with progressives from other social groups against a government that was thrashing about violently as it endured its final weeks of life. What do you do to replace it?

Marx and Engels' cryptic answer is their description of a commune, based on the one in Paris, that champions democracy. Many people in our movement point to the Marxist of "the dictatorship of the proletariat" as proof that Karl and Friedrich's vision is fundamentally undemocratic and incompatible with any acceptable social design. But this vision of "dictatorship" is much more democratic than anything we currently live under. With the exception of the bourgeoisie, which would be excluded from any decision-making body, the commune includes virtually every social group, including women (a stunning addition given the attitudes of that time). Petite-bourgeois, professionals, clerics, marginalized people all had agency within the envisioned commune. Logically, all this is directed by the proletariat but it is an inclusive leadership.

That, more or less, is it. That's all Karl and Friedrich give us on this topic. During the entire time since their death, Marxists have sought to forge societies or ideas of governance based on scant phrases in relatively obscure letters or articles or, more often, projections of what Marx and Engels would have said. In all cases, our description of what we would replace capitalist government with has fallen short. We have no consensus because we just don't know. The efforts we have made created societies that, while more sustainable than capitalist societies, are places many of us would be more comfortable supporting than living in.

The picture is infuriating because we are today in the best position in human history to design and describe a new just and sustainable society and we haven't done anything close to that.

Why is that so hard? In part, perhaps, because it requires the construction of our own separate culture, and that task has proven daunting. Maybe our left movement, among the most skilled, educated and articulate in the country's history, has been leveled and pushed backwards by the privilege that accompanies the development of those capabilities. The gap it has created between our movement leadership and the people whose lives are literally threatened every day of the week has proven very difficult to close. The hard truth is that those of us who most need a revolution don't want one, and those who want one are among the people who least need one.

That's hegemony at work. Your comfort and complacency

is illusory; your privilege ephemeral. Our task is to develop a culture that breaks through those illusions, that truly sees the long-term trends that threaten all our lives, and that posits a solution for them that defies imagination restrictions and rages against the inflexible formulas our past movement has sought to impose on us. Throw everything out the window and create a society based on what we really need...and what we really can do.

In fact, we can do what we need to. For the first time in our history, the human race has the technology needed to feed the world. We know the solutions to the climate problem. We have in place the research capability to transform many illnesses from terminal to chronic, something that's happened with many cancers. We have a remarkable system of instant, robust communication between any two points on Earth. These are abilities that were unheard of 30 years ago; they are now taken for granted. For most of my life, we would say, "We have the will to develop what we need to do this." But today we can soberly say, "We only need the will to use what we have to make this happen."

The step we need to take, however, is to actually describe this future society and make that our principal point: the thing we talk about most.

Again, all protest makes demands on the government, and that is a powerful and productive road. In fact, it's inevitable. But a true revolutionary movement is based, not only on protest, but on promise. We not only oppose the horrors we live in this society but propose a society devoid of those horrors. We pose an alternative.

The political culture of the United States and most "developed" countries, demands this. The hegemony the ruling class maintains over us will never allow us to overthrow capitalism without a clear alternative because we live in a the daily stupor of confidence in this system, almost like an abused pet. We're programmed to fear crossing the line of social change and we can't break the programming without seeing something clear and concrete over the line.

We need to sit down as a movement and figure out what we want to create and then it will be clear how to get there. Give people a solid alternative and they will make a revolution.

Marx and Engels prepared us for this moment when they made their fundamental point about people: we can see tomorrow, we can imagine its beauty and potential, we can design its elegant efficiency. We can apply the power of imagination that our forebears have constantly used to survive, to progress and to refashion this remarkable world. What we do about that is the topic for the next chapter…the one all of us are about to write. Karl and Friedrich would have encouraged us to do that with vigor and commitment.

4

Conclusion

Realizing that I'm incapable of writing some brilliant conclusion, I began thinking about how to wrap this up and decided that I'd return to my original intent: that this might be used as a kind of study tool. Not sure if that works but I've prepared a bunch of questions, one for each chapter, just in case. I was thinking maybe the people in a study group can write something in answer to each question once a week. Then get together, read what you all wrote and talk it over. Or whatever. Or just read the questions. I find that the worse person to decide how to use something is the person who actually wrote it.

Anyway, here are the questions.

Section 1 — If you could contribute something fundamental to the world tomorrow or in the near future, what would it be? Describe it and its impact.

Section 2 — An exercise — Pick a product in your house or office and trace its production/consumption country by country. Don't forget the raw materials involved in making it.

Section 3 — How much do you owe? Why? What did you spend that money on? Could you live without it?

Section 4 — That product in exercise 1 — could it have been made in the U.S.? Was it ever?

Section 5 — Make a list of what you want out of life. The basics. How much of that can a sane society deliver?

Section 6 — Talking about your specific day to day life, what parts of the "super-structure" came into contact with you today?

Section 7 — What is success in life for you...you specifically, not the entire human race? Is it possible in this society?

Section 8 — What kinds of alienation do you experience in your life? Be specific.

Section 9 — What class do you belong to? How does that affect your life?

Section 10 — What do you think we should do to combat fascism?

Section 11 — Describe the world you want to live in. Be as specific as possible and be honest about obstacles and problems.

Afterword

Alfredo Lopez, a revolutionary organizer and activist for a half century, has been a leader of the Puerto Rican Socialist Party in the U.S.; organizer of many actions, campaigns and demonstrations (including the 1974 Day of Solidarity with Puerto Rican Independence in Madison Square Garden); a founder of May First Movement Technology; author of six published books and one of the founders of Radical Elders. He is currently Senior Advisor at Media Justice.

He lives in Brooklyn, New York with his wife and life-partner, writer, educator and activist Maritza Arrastia.

www.ingramcontent.com/pod-product-compliance
Lightning Source LLC
Chambersburg PA
CBHW070034040426
42333CB00040B/1676